MznLnx

Missing Links Exam Preps

Exam Prep for

Creative Strategy in Advertising

Drewniany & Jewler, 9th Edition

The MznLnx Exam Prep is your link from the texbook and lecture to your exams.
The MznLnx Exam Preps are unauthorized and comprehensive reviews of your textbooks.

MznLnx

Rico
Publications

Exam Prep for Creative Strategy in Advertising
9th Edition
Drewniany & Jewler

Publisher: Raymond Houge
Assistant Editor: Michael Rouger
Text and Cover Designer: Lisa Buckner
Marketing Manager: Sara Swagger
Project Manager, Editorial Production: Jerry Emerson
Art Director: Vernon Lowerui

Product Manager: Dave Mason
Editorial Assitant: Rachel Guzmanji
Pedagogy: Debra Long
Cover Image: Jim Reed/Getty Images
Text and Cover Printer: City Printing, Inc.
Compositor: Media Mix, Inc.

For more information about our products, contact us at:
Dave.Mason@RicoPublications.com

For permission to use material from this text or product, submit a request online to:
Dave.Mason@RicoPublications.com

Printed in the United States
ISBN:

Contents

TO THE STUDENT

COMPREHENSIVE

The *MznLnx* Exam Prep series is designed to help you pass your exams. Editors at MznLnx review your textbooks and then prepare these practice exams to help you master the textbook material. Unlike study guides, workbooks, and practice tests provided by the texbook publisher and textbook authors, *MznLnx* gives you ***all*** of the material in each chapter in exam form, not just samples, so you can be sure to nail your exam.

MECHANICAL

The MznLnx Exam Prep series creates exams that will help you learn the subject matter as well as test you on your understanding. Each question is designed to help you master the concept. Just working through the exams, you gain an understanding of the subject--its a simple mechanical process that produces success.

INTEGRATED STUDY GUIDE AND REVIEW

MznLnx is not just a set of exams designed to test you, its also a comprehensive review of the subject content. Each exam question is also a review of the concept, making sure that you will get the answer correct without having to go to other sources of material. You learn as you go! Its the easiest way to pass an exam.

HUMOR

Studying can be tedious and dry. MznLnx's instructional design includes moderate humor within the exam questions on occassion, to break the tedium and revitalize the brain

1. A _________ is a relatively new executive level position at a corporation, company, organization typically reporting directly to the CEO or board of directors. The _________ is responsible for a brand's image, experience, and promise, and propagating it throughout all aspects of the company. The brand officer oversees marketing, advertising, design, public relations and customer service departments.
   a. Financial analyst
   b. Chief executive officer
   c. Chief brand officer
   d. Power III

2. A _________ is a collection of symbols, experiences and associations connected with a product, a service, a person or any other artifact or entity.

_________s have become increasingly important components of culture and the economy, now being described as 'cultural accessories and personal philosophies'.

Some people distinguish the psychological aspect of a _________ from the experiential aspect.

   a. Brand
   b. Brand equity
   c. Brandable software
   d. Store brand

3. In marketing and advertising, a _________ usually an advertising campaign, is aimed at appealing to. A _________ can be people of a certain age group, gender, marital status, etc. (ex: teenagers, females, single people, etc.)
   a. National brand
   b. Target audience
   c. Brand Development Index
   d. Targeted advertising

4. _________ is a form of communication that typically attempts to persuade potential customers to purchase or to consume more of a particular brand of product or service. 'While now central to the contemporary global economy and the reproduction of global production networks, it is only quite recently that _________ has been more than a marginal influence on patterns of sales and production. The formation of modern _________ was intimately bound up with the emergence of new forms of monopoly capitalism around the end of the 19th and beginning of the 20th century as one element in corporate strategies to create, organize and where possible control markets, especially for mass produced consumer goods.
   a. ADTECH
   b. Advertising
   c. AMAX
   d. ACNielsen

5. A _________ or community service announcement (CSA) is a non-commercial advertisement broadcast on radio or television, ostensibly for the public interest. _________s are intended to modify public attitudes by raising awareness about specific issues.

The most common topics of _________s are health and safety.

a. 6-3-5 Brainwriting
b. 180SearchAssistant
c. Power III
d. Public service announcement

6. A _________ is typically the attributes one associates with a brand, how the brand owner wants the consumer to perceive the brand - and by extension the branded company, organization, product or service. The brand owner will seek to bridge the gap between the _________ and the brand identity.

a. Brand equity
b. Brand loyalty
c. Status brand
d. Brand image

7. _________ is an advertisement in which a particular product specifically mentions a competitor by name for the express purpose of showing why the competitor is inferior to the product naming it.

This should not be confused with parody advertisements, where a fictional product is being advertised for the purpose of poking fun at the particular advertisement, nor should it be confused with the use of a coined brand name for the purpose of comparing the product without actually naming an actual competitor. ('Wikipedia tastes better and is less filling than the Encyclopedia Galactica.')

In the 1980s, during what has been referred to as the cola wars, soft-drink manufacturer Pepsi ran a series of advertisements where people, caught on hidden camera, in a blind taste test, chose Pepsi over rival Coca-Cola.

a. Comparative advertising
b. Cost per conversion
c. Heavy-up
d. GL-70

8. _________ is a broad label that refers to any individuals or households that use goods and services generated within the economy. The concept of a _________ is used in different contexts, so that the usage and significance of the term may vary.

A _________ is a person who uses any product or service.

a. 6-3-5 Brainwriting
b. 180SearchAssistant
c. Power III
d. Consumer

9. _________ is a rivalry between individuals, groups, nations for territory, a niche, or allocation of resources. It arises whenever two or more parties strive for a goal which cannot be shared. _________ occurs naturally between living organisms which co-exist in the same environment.
a. Price fixing
b. Price competition
c. Non-price competition
d. Competition

10. _________ is a sub-discipline and type of marketing. There are two main definitional characteristics which distinguish it from other types of marketing. The first is that it attempts to send its messages directly to consumers, without the use of intervening media.
a. Direct marketing
b. Direct Marketing Associations
c. Database marketing
d. Power III

11. _________ is defined by the American _________ Association as the activity, set of institutions, and processes for creating, communicating, delivering, and exchanging offerings that have value for customers, clients, partners, and society at large. The term developed from the original meaning which referred literally to going to market, as in shopping, or going to a market to sell goods or services.

_________ practice tends to be seen as a creative industry, which includes advertising, distribution and selling.

a. Customer acquisition management
b. Marketing
c. Product naming
d. Marketing myopia

12. _________ is a magazine, delivering news, analysis and data on marketing and media. The magazine was started as a broadsheet newspaper in Chicago in 1930. Today, its content appears in a print weekly distributed around the world and on many electronic platforms, including: AdAge.com, daily e-mail newsletters called Ad Age Daily, Ad Age's Mediaworks and Ad Age Digital; weekly newsletters such as Madison ' Vine (about branded entertainment) and Ad Age China; podcasts called Why It Matters and various videos.

a. Adweek
b. Outsert
c. Ethical Consumer
d. Advertising Age

13. _________ is a weekly American advertising trade publication that was first published in 1978. _________ covers creativity, client/agency relationships, global advertising, accounts in review, and new campaigns. During this time, it has covered several notable shifts, including cable television, the shift away from commission-based agency fees, and the Internet.
a. American Booksellers Association
b. Ethical Consumer
c. Entrepreneur magazine
d. Adweek

14. The U.S. _________ is an agency of the United States Department of Health and Human Services and is responsible for regulating and supervising the safety of foods, dietary supplements, drugs, vaccines, biological medical products, blood products, medical devices, radiation-emitting devices, veterinary products, and cosmetics. The FDA also enforces section 361 of the Public Health Service Act and the associated regulations, including sanitation requirements on interstate travel as well as specific rules for control of disease on products ranging from pet turtles to semen donations for assisted reproductive medicine techniques.

The FDA is an agency within the United States Department of Health and Human Services responsible for protecting and promoting the nation's public health.

a. 6-3-5 Brainwriting
b. Power III
c. 180SearchAssistant
d. Food and Drug Administration

15. _________ refers to 'controlling human or societal behaviour by rules or restrictions.' _________ can take many forms: legal restrictions promulgated by a government authority, self-_________, social _________, co-_________ and market _________. One can consider _________ as actions of conduct imposing sanctions (such as a fine.) This action of administrative law, or implementing regulatory law, may be contrasted with statutory or case law.
a. Rule of four
b. Non-conventional trademark
c. CAN-SPAM
d. Regulation

16. _________ , according to The American Marketing Association, is 'a planning process designed to assure that all brand contacts received by a customer or prospect for a product, service, or organization are relevant to that person and consistent over time.' (Marketing Power Dictionary)

_________ is a term used to describe a holistic approach to marketing. It aims to ensure consistency of message and the complementary use of media. The concept includes online and offline marketing channels.

a. AMAX
b. ADTECH
c. ACNielsen
d. Integrated marketing communications

17. _________ refers to messages and related media used to communicate with a market. Those who practice advertising, branding, direct marketing, graphic design, marketing, packaging, promotion, publicity, sponsorship, public relations, sales, sales promotion and online marketing are termed marketing communicators, _________ managers, or more briefly as marcom managers.

a. Merchandise
b. Marketing communication
c. Merchandising
d. Sales promotion

1. A _________ is a plan of action designed to achieve a particular goal.

_________ is different from tactics. In military terms, tactics is concerned with the conduct of an engagement while _________ is concerned with how different engagements are linked.

a. 6-3-5 Brainwriting
b. Power III
c. 180SearchAssistant
d. Strategy

2. A _________ is a collection of symbols, experiences and associations connected with a product, a service, a person or any other artifact or entity.

_________s have become increasingly important components of culture and the economy, now being described as 'cultural accessories and personal philosophies'.

Some people distinguish the psychological aspect of a _________ from the experiential aspect.

a. Store brand
b. Brandable software
c. Brand
d. Brand equity

3. A _________ is typically the attributes one associates with a brand, how the brand owner wants the consumer to perceive the brand - and by extension the branded company, organization, product or service. The brand owner will seek to bridge the gap between the _________ and the brand identity.
a. Status brand
b. Brand equity
c. Brand loyalty
d. Brand image

4. _________ is difficult to define. For example, in 1952, Alfred Kroeber and Clyde Kluckhohn compiled a list of 164 definitions of '_________' in _________: A Critical Review of Concepts and Definitions. However, the word '_________' is most commonly used in three basic senses:

- excellence of taste in the fine arts and humanities
- an integrated pattern of human knowledge, belief, and behavior that depends upon the capacity for symbolic thought and social learning
- the set of shared attitudes, values, goals, and practices that characterizes an institution, organization or group.

When the concept first emerged in eighteenth- and nineteenth-century Europe, it connoted a process of cultivation or improvement, as in agriculture or horticulture. In the nineteenth century, it came to refer first to the betterment or refinement of the individual, especially through education, and then to the fulfillment of national aspirations or ideals.

a. Culture
b. AStore
c. Albert Einstein
d. African Americans

5. _________ , according to The American Marketing Association, is 'a planning process designed to assure that all brand contacts received by a customer or prospect for a product, service, or organization are relevant to that person and consistent over time.' (Marketing Power Dictionary)

_________ is a term used to describe a holistic approach to marketing. It aims to ensure consistency of message and the complementary use of media. The concept includes online and offline marketing channels.

a. Integrated marketing communications
b. ADTECH
c. ACNielsen
d. AMAX

6. _________ is defined by the American _________ Association as the activity, set of institutions, and processes for creating, communicating, delivering, and exchanging offerings that have value for customers, clients, partners, and society at large. The term developed from the original meaning which referred literally to going to market, as in shopping, or going to a market to sell goods or services.

_________ practice tends to be seen as a creative industry, which includes advertising, distribution and selling.

a. Product naming
b. Marketing
c. Customer acquisition management
d. Marketing myopia

7. _________ refers to messages and related media used to communicate with a market. Those who practice advertising, branding, direct marketing, graphic design, marketing, packaging, promotion, publicity, sponsorship, public relations, sales, sales promotion and online marketing are termed marketing communicators, _________ managers, or more briefly as marcom managers.

a. Merchandising
b. Merchandise
c. Marketing communication
d. Sales promotion

8. A _________ or trade mark, identified by the symbols â„¢ (not yet registered) and Â® (registered) business organization or other legal entity to identify that the products and/or services to consumers with which the _________ appears originate from a unique source of origin, and to distinguish its products or services from those of other entities. A _________ is a type of intellectual property, and typically a name, word, phrase, logo, symbol, design, image, or a combination of these elements. There is also a range of non-conventional _________s comprising marks which do not fall into these standard categories.
a. Trademark
b. Power III
c. Risk management
d. 180SearchAssistant

9. Once trademark rights are established in a particular jurisdiction, these rights are generally only enforceable in that jurisdiction, a quality which is sometimes known as territoriality. However, there is a range of international _________ and systems which facilitate the protection of trademarks in more than one jurisdiction

To avoid conflicts with earlier trademark rights, it is highly recommended to conduct trademark searches before the trademarks office (or 'trademarks registry') of a particular jurisdiction--e.g. US Patent and Trademark Office.

a. Self branding
b. Supreme Court of the United States
c. Trademark laws
d. Sigg bottles

10. _________ is a form of intellectual property which gives the creator of an original work exclusive rights for a certain time period in relation to that work, including its publication, distribution and adaptation; after which time the work is said to enter the public domain. _________ applies to any expressible form of an idea or information that is substantive and discrete. Some jurisdictions also recognize 'moral rights' of the creator of a work, such as the right to be credited for the work.
a. Copyright
b. Reasonable person standard
c. Celler-Kefauver Act
d. Collective mark

11. _________ is the practice of managing the flow of information between an organization and its publics. _________ - often referred to as _________ - gains an organization or individual exposure to their audiences using topics of public interest and news items that do not require direct payment. Because _________ places exposure in credible third-party outlets, it offers a third-party legitimacy that advertising does not have.

a. Power III
b. Graphic communication
c. Symbolic analysis
d. Public Relations

1. _________ is defined by the American _________ Association as the activity, set of institutions, and processes for creating, communicating, delivering, and exchanging offerings that have value for customers, clients, partners, and society at large. The term developed from the original meaning which referred literally to going to market, as in shopping, or going to a market to sell goods or services.

_________ practice tends to be seen as a creative industry, which includes advertising, distribution and selling.

a. Marketing myopia
b. Customer acquisition management
c. Product naming
d. Marketing

2. _________ refers to messages and related media used to communicate with a market. Those who practice advertising, branding, direct marketing, graphic design, marketing, packaging, promotion, publicity, sponsorship, public relations, sales, sales promotion and online marketing are termed marketing communicators, _________ managers, or more briefly as marcom managers.
a. Sales promotion
b. Merchandise
c. Merchandising
d. Marketing communication

3. A _________ is the space, actual or metaphorical, in which a market operates. The term is also used in a trademark law context to denote the actual consumer environment, ie. the 'real world' in which products and services are provided and consumed.
a. Power III
b. 6-3-5 Brainwriting
c. 180SearchAssistant
d. Marketplace

4. _________ or _________ data refers to selected population characteristics as used in government, marketing or opinion research, or the _________ profiles used in such research. Note the distinction from the term 'demography' Commonly-used _________ include race, age, income, disabilities, mobility (in terms of travel time to work or number of vehicles available), educational attainment, home ownership, employment status, and even location.
a. African Americans
b. Albert Einstein
c. AStore
d. Demographic

5. _________ is a form of communication that typically attempts to persuade potential customers to purchase or to consume more of a particular brand of product or service. 'While now central to the contemporary global economy and the reproduction of global production networks, it is only quite recently that _________ has been more than a marginal influence on patterns of sales and production. The formation of modern _________ was intimately bound up with the emergence of new forms of monopoly capitalism around the end of the 19th and beginning of the 20th century as one element in corporate strategies to create, organize and where possible control markets, especially for mass produced consumer goods.

a. ACNielsen
b. Advertising
c. AMAX
d. ADTECH

6. _________s is the social science that studies the production, distribution, and consumption of goods and services. The term _________s comes from the Ancient Greek οἰκονομία from οἶκος (oikos, 'house') + νόμος (nomos, 'custom' or 'law'), hence 'rules of the house(hold)'. Current _________ models developed out of the broader field of political economy in the late 19th century, owing to a desire to use an empirical approach more akin to the physical sciences.

a. Industrial organization
b. ACNielsen
c. ADTECH
d. Economic

7. _________ is the increase in the amount of the goods and services produced by an economy over time. It is conventionally measured as the percent rate of increase in real gross domestic product, or real GDP. Growth is usually calculated in real terms, i.e. inflation-adjusted terms, in order to net out the effect of inflation on the price of the goods and services produced.

a. Economic Growth
b. AMAX
c. ACNielsen
d. ADTECH

8. _________ is a sub-discipline and type of marketing. There are two main definitional characteristics which distinguish it from other types of marketing. The first is that it attempts to send its messages directly to consumers, without the use of intervening media.

a. Direct marketing
b. Direct Marketing Associations
c. Power III
d. Database marketing

9. _________ is a magazine, delivering news, analysis and data on marketing and media. The magazine was started as a broadsheet newspaper in Chicago in 1930. Today, its content appears in a print weekly distributed around the world and on many electronic platforms, including: AdAge.com, daily e-mail newsletters called Ad Age Daily, Ad Age's Mediaworks and Ad Age Digital; weekly newsletters such as Madison ' Vine (about branded entertainment) and Ad Age China; podcasts called Why It Matters and various videos.

a. Adweek
b. Advertising Age
c. Ethical Consumer
d. Outsert

10. _________ is a weekly American advertising trade publication that was first published in 1978. _________ covers creativity, client/agency relationships, global advertising, accounts in review, and new campaigns. During this time, it has covered several notable shifts, including cable television, the shift away from commission-based agency fees, and the Internet.

a. Ethical Consumer
b. Entrepreneur magazine
c. American Booksellers Association
d. Adweek

1. Many institutions make a distinction between circulating _________ and collecting _________ Many modern _________ are a mixture of both, as they contain a general collection for circulation, and a reference collection which is often more specialized, as well as restricted to the library premises.

Also, the governments of most major countries support national _________.

a. 6-3-5 Brainwriting
b. Power III
c. Libraries
d. 180SearchAssistant

2. _________ refer to a collection of facts usually collected as the result of experience, observation or experiment or a set of premises. This may consist of numbers, words particularly as measurements or observations of a set of variables. _________ are often viewed as a lowest level of abstraction from which information and knowledge are derived.
a. Sample size
b. Pearson product-moment correlation coefficient
c. Data
d. Mean

3. A _________ is a structured collection of records or data that is stored in a computer system. The structure is achieved by organizing the data according to a _________ model. The model in most common use today is the relational model.
a. Power III
b. 180SearchAssistant
c. 6-3-5 Brainwriting
d. Database

4. _________ is an advertisement in which a particular product specifically mentions a competitor by name for the express purpose of showing why the competitor is inferior to the product naming it.

This should not be confused with parody advertisements, where a fictional product is being advertised for the purpose of poking fun at the particular advertisement, nor should it be confused with the use of a coined brand name for the purpose of comparing the product without actually naming an actual competitor. ('Wikipedia tastes better and is less filling than the Encyclopedia Galactica.')

In the 1980s, during what has been referred to as the cola wars, soft-drink manufacturer Pepsi ran a series of advertisements where people, caught on hidden camera, in a blind taste test, chose Pepsi over rival Coca-Cola.

a. GL-70
b. Comparative advertising
c. Heavy-up
d. Cost per conversion

5. _________ is either an activity of a living being (such as a human), consisting of receiving knowledge of the outside world through the senses, or the recording of data using scientific instruments. The term may also refer to any datum collected during this activity.

The scientific method requires _________s of nature to formulate and test hypotheses.

a. Observation
b. AMAX
c. ADTECH
d. ACNielsen

6. _________ involves the collection of data that does not already exist. This can be through numerous forms, including questionnaires and telephone interviews amongst others. This information may be collected in things like questionnaires, magazines, and Interviews

The term is widely used in market research and competitive intelligence.

a. Brand infiltration
b. Bitcom
c. Blitz QFD
d. Primary research

7. A _________ is a form of qualitative research in which a group of people are asked about their attitude towards a product, service, concept, advertisement, idea, or packaging. Questions are asked in an interactive group setting where participants are free to talk with other group members.

Ernest Dichter originated the idea of having a 'group therapy' for products and this process is what became known as a _________.

a. Marketing research process
b. Logit analysis
c. Cross tabulation
d. Focus group

8. _________ is a genre of writing that uses fieldwork to provide a descriptive study of human societies. _________ presents the results of a holistic research method founded on the idea that a system's properties cannot necessarily be accurately understood independently of each other. The genre has both formal and historical connections to travel writing and colonial office reports.

a. ACNielsen
b. Ethnography
c. AMAX
d. ADTECH

1. A _________ is a plan of action designed to achieve a particular goal.

_________ is different from tactics. In military terms, tactics is concerned with the conduct of an engagement while _________ is concerned with how different engagements are linked.

a. 6-3-5 Brainwriting
b. Strategy
c. Power III
d. 180SearchAssistant

2. _________ is a rivalry between individuals, groups, nations for territory, a niche, or allocation of resources. It arises whenever two or more parties strive for a goal which cannot be shared. _________ occurs naturally between living organisms which co-exist in the same environment.

a. Price competition
b. Competition
c. Price fixing
d. Non-price competition

3. _________ in organizations and public policy is both the organizational process of creating and maintaining a plan; and the psychological process of thinking about the activities required to create a desired goal on some scale. As such, it is a fundamental property of intelligent behavior. This thought process is essential to the creation and refinement of a plan, or integration of it with other plans, that is, it combines forecasting of developments with the preparation of scenarios of how to react to them.

a. Power III
b. 6-3-5 Brainwriting
c. Planning
d. 180SearchAssistant

4. _________ is a market coverage strategy in which a firm decides to ignore market segment differences and go after the whole market with one offer.it is type of marketing (or attempting to sell through persuasion) of a product to a wide audience. The idea is to broadcast a message that will reach the largest number of people possible. Traditionally _________ has focused on radio, television and newspapers as the medium used to reach this broad audience.

a. Mass marketing
b. Marketspace
c. Cyberdoc
d. Business-to-consumer

1. A _________ is a plan of action designed to achieve a particular goal.

_________ is different from tactics. In military terms, tactics is concerned with the conduct of an engagement while _________ is concerned with how different engagements are linked.

a. 6-3-5 Brainwriting
b. 180SearchAssistant
c. Power III
d. Strategy

2. A _________ is a collection of symbols, experiences and associations connected with a product, a service, a person or any other artifact or entity.

_________s have become increasingly important components of culture and the economy, now being described as 'cultural accessories and personal philosophies'.

Some people distinguish the psychological aspect of a _________ from the experiential aspect.

a. Brandable software
b. Store brand
c. Brand equity
d. Brand

3. In marketing and advertising, a _________ usually an advertising campaign, is aimed at appealing to. A _________ can be people of a certain age group, gender, marital status, etc. (ex: teenagers, females, single people, etc.)
a. Brand Development Index
b. Targeted advertising
c. National brand
d. Target audience

4. The term _________, invented to replace the older gender-based terms, is a typical example of a gender-neutral neologism.

In the present media-sensitive world, many organizations are increasingly likely to employ professionals who have received formal training in journalism, communications, public relations and public affairs in this role in order to ensure that public announcements are made in the most appropriate fashion and through the most appropriate channels to maximize the impact of favorable messages, and to minimize the impact of unfavorable messages. Popular local and national sports stars are often chosen as spokespeople for commercial advertising.

a. Power III
b. Spokesperson
c. 180SearchAssistant
d. Professional services

5. _________ is a group creativity technique designed to generate a large number of ideas for the solution of a problem. The method was first popularized in the late 1930s by Alex Faickney Osborn in a book called Applied Imagination. Osborn proposed that groups could double their creative output with _________.
a. Albert Einstein
b. Brainstorming
c. African Americans
d. AStore

6. A _________ is a relatively new executive level position at a corporation, company, organization typically reporting directly to the CEO or board of directors. The _________ is responsible for a brand's image, experience, and promise, and propagating it throughout all aspects of the company. The brand officer oversees marketing, advertising, design, public relations and customer service departments.
a. Chief brand officer
b. Power III
c. Financial analyst
d. Chief executive officer

1. A _________ is a list of the general tasks and responsibilities of a position. Typically, it also includes to whom the position reports, specifications such as the qualifications needed by the person in the job, salary range for the position, etc. A _________ is usually developed by conducting a job analysis, which includes examining the tasks and sequences of tasks necessary to perform the job.
   a. Job description
   b. Power III
   c. 180SearchAssistant
   d. 6-3-5 Brainwriting

2. A _________ is a collection of symbols, experiences and associations connected with a product, a service, a person or any other artifact or entity.

_________s have become increasingly important components of culture and the economy, now being described as 'cultural accessories and personal philosophies'.

Some people distinguish the psychological aspect of a _________ from the experiential aspect.

   a. Store brand
   b. Brand
   c. Brand equity
   d. Brandable software

3. _________ is a form of communication that typically attempts to persuade potential customers to purchase or to consume more of a particular brand of product or service. 'While now central to the contemporary global economy and the reproduction of global production networks, it is only quite recently that _________ has been more than a marginal influence on patterns of sales and production. The formation of modern _________ was intimately bound up with the emergence of new forms of monopoly capitalism around the end of the 19th and beginning of the 20th century as one element in corporate strategies to create, organize and where possible control markets, especially for mass produced consumer goods.
   a. ACNielsen
   b. AMAX
   c. ADTECH
   d. Advertising

4. _________ is a weekly American advertising trade publication that was first published in 1978. _________ covers creativity, client/agency relationships, global advertising, accounts in review, and new campaigns. During this time, it has covered several notable shifts, including cable television, the shift away from commission-based agency fees, and the Internet.

a. American Booksellers Association

b. Ethical Consumer

c. Adweek

d. Entrepreneur magazine

1. A _________ is a list of the general tasks and responsibilities of a position. Typically, it also includes to whom the position reports, specifications such as the qualifications needed by the person in the job, salary range for the position, etc. A _________ is usually developed by conducting a job analysis, which includes examining the tasks and sequences of tasks necessary to perform the job.

   a. 180SearchAssistant
   b. Power III
   c. 6-3-5 Brainwriting
   d. Job description

2. _________ is the study of the Earth and its lands, features, inhabitants, and phenomena. A literal translation would be 'to describe or write about the Earth'. The first person to use the word '_________' was Eratosthenes .

   a. Power III
   b. 180SearchAssistant
   c. 6-3-5 Brainwriting
   d. Geography

3. A number of different _________s are indicated below.

- Randomized controlled trial
  - Double-blind randomized trial
  - Single-blind randomized trial
  - Non-blind trial
- Nonrandomized trial (quasi-experiment)
  - Interrupted time series design (measures on a sample or a series of samples from the same population are obtained several times before and after a manipulated event or a naturally occurring event) - considered a type of quasi-experiment

- Cohort study
  - Prospective cohort
  - Retrospective cohort
  - Time series study
- Case-control study
  - Nested case-control study
- Cross-sectional study
  - Community survey (a type of cross-sectional study)

When choosing a _________, many factors must be taken into account. Different types of studies are subject to different types of bias. For example, recall bias is likely to occur in cross-sectional or case-control studies where subjects are asked to recall exposure to risk factors.

a. Longitudinal studies
b. Power III
c. 180SearchAssistant
d. Study design

4. A _________ is a structured collection of records or data that is stored in a computer system. The structure is achieved by organizing the data according to a _________ model. The model in most common use today is the relational model.
a. 6-3-5 Brainwriting
b. 180SearchAssistant
c. Power III
d. Database

5. _________ is a form of communication that typically attempts to persuade potential customers to purchase or to consume more of a particular brand of product or service. 'While now central to the contemporary global economy and the reproduction of global production networks, it is only quite recently that _________ has been more than a marginal influence on patterns of sales and production. The formation of modern _________ was intimately bound up with the emergence of new forms of monopoly capitalism around the end of the 19th and beginning of the 20th century as one element in corporate strategies to create, organize and where possible control markets, especially for mass produced consumer goods.
a. ACNielsen
b. Advertising
c. AMAX
d. ADTECH

1. _________ is a form of communication that typically attempts to persuade potential customers to purchase or to consume more of a particular brand of product or service. 'While now central to the contemporary global economy and the reproduction of global production networks, it is only quite recently that _________ has been more than a marginal influence on patterns of sales and production. The formation of modern _________ was intimately bound up with the emergence of new forms of monopoly capitalism around the end of the 19th and beginning of the 20th century as one element in corporate strategies to create, organize and where possible control markets, especially for mass produced consumer goods.
   a. ADTECH
   b. AMAX
   c. ACNielsen
   d. Advertising

2. _________ is a sub-discipline and type of marketing. There are two main definitional characteristics which distinguish it from other types of marketing. The first is that it attempts to send its messages directly to consumers, without the use of intervening media.
   a. Power III
   b. Direct Marketing Associations
   c. Database marketing
   d. Direct marketing

3. _________ is defined by the American _________ Association as the activity, set of institutions, and processes for creating, communicating, delivering, and exchanging offerings that have value for customers, clients, partners, and society at large. The term developed from the original meaning which referred literally to going to market, as in shopping, or going to a market to sell goods or services.

_________ practice tends to be seen as a creative industry, which includes advertising, distribution and selling.

   a. Marketing myopia
   b. Marketing
   c. Product naming
   d. Customer acquisition management

4. A _________ is a form of advertising via the medium of radio. Airtime is purchased from a station or network in exchange for airing the commercials.

The first _________ is credited to WEAF, New York on August 28, 1922 for the Queensboro real estate corporation.

a. Ghost sign
b. Transit media
c. Costco Connection
d. Radio commercial

5. A _________ is a memorable slogan, set to an engaging melody, mainly broadcast on radio and sometimes on television commercials.

.

The _________ had no definitive debut: its infiltration of the radio was more of an evolutionary process than a sudden innovation. Product advertisements with a musical tilt can be traced back to 1923, around the same time commercial radio came to the public.

a. Non-commercial advertising
b. Link flooding
c. Custom media
d. Jingle

1. _________ is a sub-discipline and type of marketing. There are two main definitional characteristics which distinguish it from other types of marketing. The first is that it attempts to send its messages directly to consumers, without the use of intervening media.

a. Database marketing
b. Power III
c. Direct Marketing Associations
d. Direct marketing

1. _________ is a sub-discipline and type of marketing. There are two main definitional characteristics which distinguish it from other types of marketing. The first is that it attempts to send its messages directly to consumers, without the use of intervening media.

a. Power III
b. Direct Marketing Associations
c. Database marketing
d. Direct marketing

2. _________ is defined by the American _________ Association as the activity, set of institutions, and processes for creating, communicating, delivering, and exchanging offerings that have value for customers, clients, partners, and society at large. The term developed from the original meaning which referred literally to going to market, as in shopping, or going to a market to sell goods or services.

_________ practice tends to be seen as a creative industry, which includes advertising, distribution and selling.

a. Marketing myopia
b. Product naming
c. Marketing
d. Customer acquisition management

3. _________ is anything that is intended to save time, energy or frustration. A _________ store at a petrol station, for example, sells items that have nothing to do with gasoline/petrol, but it saves the consumer from having to go to a grocery store. '_________' is a very relative term and its meaning tends to change over time.

a. Marketing buzz
b. Demographic profile
c. MaxDiff
d. Convenience

4. _________ is the examining of goods or services from retailers with the intent to purchase at that time. _________ is an activity of selection and/or purchase. In some contexts it is considered a leisure activity as well as an economic one.

a. Shopping
b. Discount store
c. Khodebshchik
d. Hawkers

5. _________ is a form of communication that typically attempts to persuade potential customers to purchase or to consume more of a particular brand of product or service. 'While now central to the contemporary global economy and the reproduction of global production networks, it is only quite recently that _________ has been more than a marginal influence on patterns of sales and production. The formation of modern _________ was intimately bound up with the emergence of new forms of monopoly capitalism around the end of the 19th and beginning of the 20th century as one element in corporate strategies to create, organize and where possible control markets, especially for mass produced consumer goods.

a. AMAX
b. Advertising
c. ACNielsen
d. ADTECH

6. A _________ is a structured collection of records or data that is stored in a computer system. The structure is achieved by organizing the data according to a _________ model. The model in most common use today is the relational model.

a. 180SearchAssistant
b. 6-3-5 Brainwriting
c. Power III
d. Database

7. A _________ is a relatively new executive level position at a corporation, company, organization typically reporting directly to the CEO or board of directors. The _________ is responsible for a brand's image, experience, and promise, and propagating it throughout all aspects of the company. The brand officer oversees marketing, advertising, design, public relations and customer service departments.

a. Financial analyst
b. Power III
c. Chief executive officer
d. Chief brand officer

8. In marketing and advertising, a _________ usually an advertising campaign, is aimed at appealing to. A _________ can be people of a certain age group, gender, marital status, etc. (ex: teenagers, females, single people, etc.)

a. National brand
b. Target audience
c. Targeted advertising
d. Brand Development Index

9. The most important feature of a contract is that one party makes an _________ for an arrangement that another accepts. This can be called a 'concurrence of wills' or 'ad idem' (meeting of the minds) of two or more parties. The concept is somewhat contested.

a. ADTECH
b. AMAX
c. ACNielsen
d. Offer

10. An _________ is a series of advertisement messages that share a single idea and theme which make up an integrated marketing communication (IMC.) _________s appear in different media across a specific time frame.

The critical part of making an _________ is determining a campaign theme, as it sets the tone for the individual advertisements and other forms of marketing communications that will be used.

a. ACNielsen
b. Advertising Campaign
c. AMAX
d. ADTECH

11. _________ is a form of direct marketing which uses electronic mail as a means of communicating commercial or fundraising messages to an audience. In its broadest sense, every e-mail sent to a potential or current customer could be considered _________. However, the term is usually used to refer to:

- sending e-mails with the purpose of enhancing the relationship of a merchant with its current or previous customers and to encourage customer loyalty and repeat business,
- sending e-mails with the purpose of acquiring new customers or convincing current customers to purchase something immediately,
- adding advertisements to e-mails sent by other companies to their customers, and
- sending e-mails over the Internet, as e-mail did and does exist outside the Internet (e.g., network e-mail and FIDO.)

Researchers estimate that United States firms alone spent US$400 million on _________ in 2006.

_________ is popular with companies for several reasons:

- A mailing list provides the ability to distribute information to a wide range of specific, potential customers at a relatively low cost.
- Compared to other media investments such as direct mail or printed newsletters, e-mail is less expensive.
- An exact return on investment can be tracked ('track to basket') and has proven to be high when done properly. _________ is often reported as second only to search marketing as the most effective online marketing tactic.
- The delivery time for an e-mail message is short (i.e., seconds or minutes) as compared to a mailed advertisement (i.e., one or more days.)
- An advertiser is able to 'push' the message to its audience, as opposed to website-based advertising, which relies on a customer to visit that website.
- It is possible to impress the target audience using various unique fonts and formats. This will help in making the email messages more appealing and sweet.
- E-mail messages are easy to track. An advertiser can track users via autoresponders, web bugs, bounce messages, unsubscribe requests, read receipts, click-throughs, etc. These mechanisms can be used to measure open rates, positive or negative responses, and to correlate sales with marketing.
- Advertisers can generate repeat business affordably and automatically.
- Advertisers can reach substantial numbers of e-mail subscribers who have opted in (i.e., consented) to receive e-mail communications on subjects of interest to them.
- Over half of Internet users check or send e-mail on a typical day.
- Specific types of interaction with messages can trigger (1) other messages to be delivered automatically, or (2) other events, such as updating the profile of the recipient to indicate a specific interest category.
- _________ is paper-free (i.e., 'green'.)

Many companies use _________ to communicate with existing customers, but many other companies send unsolicited bulk e-mail, also known as spam.

Internet system administrators have always considered themselves responsible for dealing with 'abuse of the net', but not 'abuse on the net'.

a. Audience Screening
b. Online shopping rewards
c. Enterprise Search Marketing
d. E-mail Marketing

1. _________ is a rivalry between individuals, groups, nations for territory, a niche, or allocation of resources. It arises whenever two or more parties strive for a goal which cannot be shared. _________ occurs naturally between living organisms which co-exist in the same environment.

a. Non-price competition
b. Price fixing
c. Price competition
d. Competition

2. _________ in organizations and public policy is both the organizational process of creating and maintaining a plan; and the psychological process of thinking about the activities required to create a desired goal on some scale. As such, it is a fundamental property of intelligent behavior. This thought process is essential to the creation and refinement of a plan, or integration of it with other plans, that is, it combines forecasting of developments with the preparation of scenarios of how to react to them.

a. 180SearchAssistant
b. Power III
c. 6-3-5 Brainwriting
d. Planning

3. A _________ or banner ad is a form of advertising on the World Wide Web. This form of online advertising entails embedding an advertisement into a web page. It is intended to attract traffic to a website by linking to the website of the advertiser.

a. Consumer privacy
b. Spamvertising
c. Disintermediation
d. Web banner

4. _________ is a form of communication that typically attempts to persuade potential customers to purchase or to consume more of a particular brand of product or service. 'While now central to the contemporary global economy and the reproduction of global production networks, it is only quite recently that _________ has been more than a marginal influence on patterns of sales and production. The formation of modern _________ was intimately bound up with the emergence of new forms of monopoly capitalism around the end of the 19th and beginning of the 20th century as one element in corporate strategies to create, organize and where possible control markets, especially for mass produced consumer goods.

a. ACNielsen
b. AMAX
c. Advertising
d. ADTECH

1. A _________ is a collection of symbols, experiences and associations connected with a product, a service, a person or any other artifact or entity.

_________s have become increasingly important components of culture and the economy, now being described as 'cultural accessories and personal philosophies'.

Some people distinguish the psychological aspect of a _________ from the experiential aspect.

a. Brand equity
b. Brand
c. Store brand
d. Brandable software

2. _________ is a broad label that refers to any individuals or households that use goods and services generated within the economy. The concept of a _________ is used in different contexts, so that the usage and significance of the term may vary.

A _________ is a person who uses any product or service.

a. Power III
b. 180SearchAssistant
c. 6-3-5 Brainwriting
d. Consumer

3. _________ , according to The American Marketing Association, is 'a planning process designed to assure that all brand contacts received by a customer or prospect for a product, service, or organization are relevant to that person and consistent over time.' (Marketing Power Dictionary)

_________ is a term used to describe a holistic approach to marketing. It aims to ensure consistency of message and the complementary use of media. The concept includes online and offline marketing channels.

a. AMAX
b. Integrated marketing communications
c. ADTECH
d. ACNielsen

4. _________ is defined by the American _________ Association as the activity, set of institutions, and processes for creating, communicating, delivering, and exchanging offerings that have value for customers, clients, partners, and society at large. The term developed from the original meaning which referred literally to going to market, as in shopping, or going to a market to sell goods or services.

_________ practice tends to be seen as a creative industry, which includes advertising, distribution and selling.

a. Customer acquisition management
b. Product naming
c. Marketing
d. Marketing myopia

5. _________ refers to messages and related media used to communicate with a market. Those who practice advertising, branding, direct marketing, graphic design, marketing, packaging, promotion, publicity, sponsorship, public relations, sales, sales promotion and online marketing are termed marketing communicators, _________ managers, or more briefly as marcom managers.

a. Sales promotion
b. Merchandise
c. Merchandising
d. Marketing communication

6. _________ involves disseminating information about a product, product line, brand, or company. It is one of the four key aspects of the marketing mix. (The other three elements are product marketing, pricing, and distribution). P>_________ is generally sub-divided into two parts:

- Above the line _________: Promotion in the media (e.g. TV, radio, newspapers, Internet and Mobile Phones) in which the advertiser pays an advertising agency to place the ad
- Below the line _________: All other _________. Much of this is intended to be subtle enough for the consumer to be unaware that _________ is taking place. E.g. sponsorship, product placement, endorsements, sales _________, merchandising, direct mail, personal selling, public relations, trade shows

a. Davie Brown Index
b. Bottling lines
c. Promotion
d. Cashmere Agency

7. _________ is one of the four aspects of promotional mix. (The other three parts of the promotional mix are advertising, personal selling, and publicity/public relations.) Media and non-media marketing communication are employed for a pre-determined, limited time to increase consumer demand, stimulate market demand or improve product availability.

a. New Media Strategies
b. Merchandise
c. Sales promotion
d. Marketing communication

8. In the United States consumer sales promotions known as _________ or simply sweeps (both single and plural) have become associated with marketing promotions targeted toward both generating enthusiasm and providing incentive reactions among customers by enticing consumers to submit free entries into drawings of chance (and not skill) that are tied to product or service awareness wherein the featured prizes are given away by sponsoring companies. Prizes can vary in value from less than one dollar to more than one million U.S. dollars and can be in the form of cash, cars, homes, electronics, etc.

_________ frequently have eligibility limited by international, national, state, local, or other geographical factors.

a. Claritas Prizm
b. Market segment
c. Commercial planning
d. Sweepstakes

9. In marketing a _________ is a ticket or document that can be exchanged for a financial discount or rebate when purchasing a product. Customarily, _________s are issued by manufacturers of consumer packaged goods or by retailers, to be used in retail stores as a part of sales promotions. They are often widely distributed through mail, magazines, newspapers, the Internet, and mobile devices such as cell phones.
a. Merchandising
b. Merchandise
c. Marketing communication
d. Coupon

10. _________ is that part of statistical practice concerned with the selection of individual observations intended to yield some knowledge about a population of concern, especially for the purposes of statistical inference. Each observation measures one or more properties (weight, location, etc.) of an observable entity enumerated to distinguish objects or individuals.
a. AStore
b. Sampling
c. Sports Marketing Group
d. Richard Buckminster 'Bucky' Fuller

11. A _________ is an amount paid by way of reduction, return, or refund on what has already been paid or contributed. It is a type of sales promotion marketers use primarily as incentives or supplements to product sales. The mail-in _________ is the most common.

a. Lifestyle city
b. Personalization
c. Strand
d. Rebate

12. _________ is a form of communication that typically attempts to persuade potential customers to purchase or to consume more of a particular brand of product or service. 'While now central to the contemporary global economy and the reproduction of global production networks, it is only quite recently that _________ has been more than a marginal influence on patterns of sales and production. The formation of modern _________ was intimately bound up with the emergence of new forms of monopoly capitalism around the end of the 19th and beginning of the 20th century as one element in corporate strategies to create, organize and where possible control markets, especially for mass produced consumer goods.

a. ACNielsen
b. AMAX
c. ADTECH
d. Advertising

13. The business terms _________ and pull originated in the logistic and supply chain management, but are also widely used in marketing.

A _________-pull-system in business describes the move of a product or information between two subjects. On markets the consumers usually 'pulls' the goods or information they demand for their needs, while the offerers or suppliers '_________es' them toward the consumers.

a. Completely randomized designs
b. Gold Key Matching Service
c. Push
d. Manufacturers' representatives

14. _________ is a sub-discipline and type of marketing. There are two main definitional characteristics which distinguish it from other types of marketing. The first is that it attempts to send its messages directly to consumers, without the use of intervening media.

a. Direct Marketing Associations
b. Database marketing
c. Power III
d. Direct marketing

15. The _________ is an English-language international daily newspaper published by Dow Jones ' Company in New York City with Asian and European editions. As of 2007, It has a worldwide daily circulation of more than 2 million, with approximately 931,000 paying online subscribers. It was the largest-circulation newspaper in the United States until November 2003, when it was surpassed by USA Today.

a. Wall Street Journal
b. 6-3-5 Brainwriting
c. Power III
d. 180SearchAssistant

16. _________ is the practice of managing the flow of information between an organization and its publics. _________ - often referred to as _________ - gains an organization or individual exposure to their audiences using topics of public interest and news items that do not require direct payment. Because _________ places exposure in credible third-party outlets, it offers a third-party legitimacy that advertising does not have.

a. Public relations
b. Symbolic analysis
c. Graphic communication
d. Power III

17. _________ is the process by which an organization deals with any major unpredictable event that threatens to harm the organization, its stakeholders, or the general public. Three elements are common to most definitions of crisis: (a) a threat to the organization, (b) the element of surprise, and (c) a short decision time.

Whereas risk management involves assessing potential threats and finding the best ways to avoid those threats, _________ involves dealing with the disasters after they have occurred.

a. Performance measurement
b. Voice of the customer
c. Product marketing
d. Crisis management

18. _________ refers to articles of merchandise that are used in marketing and communication programs. These items are usually imprinted with a company's name, logo or slogan, and given away at trade shows, conferences, and as part of guerrilla marketing campaigns.

Almost anything can be branded with a company's name or logo and used for promotion.

a. Transpromotional
b. Testimonial
c. Roll-in
d. Promotional products

19. The _________ is a professional association for marketers. As of 2008 it had approximately 40,000 members. There are collegiate chapters on 250 campuses.
a. American Marketing Association
b. AMAX
c. ACNielsen
d. ADTECH

20. _________ refers to a type of marketing involving the cooperative efforts of a 'for profit' business and a non-profit organization for mutual benefit. The term is sometimes used more broadly and generally to refer to any type of marketing effort for social and other charitable causes, including in-house marketing efforts by non-profit organizations. Cause marketing differs from corporate giving (philanthropy) as the latter generally involves a specific donation that is tax deductible, while cause marketing is a marketing relationship generally not based on a donation.
a. Digital marketing
b. Global marketing
c. Diversity marketing
d. Cause-related marketing

21. _________ is an unconventional system of promotions that relies on time, energy and imagination rather than a big marketing budget. Typically, _________ tactics are unexpected and unconventional; consumers are targeted in unexpected places, which can make the idea that's being marketed memorable, generate buzz, and even spread virally. The term was coined and defined by Jay Conrad Levinson in his 1984 book _________.
a. Diversity marketing
b. Digital marketing
c. Cause-related Marketing
d. Guerrilla marketing

22. _________ is a relatively new form of advertising medium that blurs conventional distinctions between what constitutes advertising and what constitutes entertainment. _________ is essentially a fusion of the two into one product intended to be distributed as entertainment content, albeit with a highly branded quality. _________, unlike conventional forms of entertainment content, is generally funded entirely by a brand or corporation rather than, for example, a Movie studio or a group of producers.

a. Power III
b. Branded content
c. 6-3-5 Brainwriting
d. 180SearchAssistant

23. _________ is a form of advertisement, where branded goods or services are placed in a context usually devoid of ads, such as movies, the story line of television shows Broadcasting ' Cable reported, 'Two thirds of advertisers employ 'branded entertainment'--_________--with the vast majority of that (80%) in commercial TV programming.' The story, based on a survey by the Association of National Advertisers, added, 'Reasons for using in-show plugs varied from 'stronger emotional connection' to better dovetailing with relevant content, to targetting a specific group.'

_________ became common in the 1980s, but can be traced back to the nineteenth century in publishing.

a. 180SearchAssistant
b. Power III
c. 6-3-5 Brainwriting
d. Product placement

1. _________ is a form of communication that typically attempts to persuade potential customers to purchase or to consume more of a particular brand of product or service. 'While now central to the contemporary global economy and the reproduction of global production networks, it is only quite recently that _________ has been more than a marginal influence on patterns of sales and production. The formation of modern _________ was intimately bound up with the emergence of new forms of monopoly capitalism around the end of the 19th and beginning of the 20th century as one element in corporate strategies to create, organize and where possible control markets, especially for mass produced consumer goods.

a. ACNielsen
b. ADTECH
c. AMAX
d. Advertising

2. An _________ is a series of advertisement messages that share a single idea and theme which make up an integrated marketing communication (IMC.) _________s appear in different media across a specific time frame.

The critical part of making an _________ is determining a campaign theme, as it sets the tone for the individual advertisements and other forms of marketing communications that will be used.

a. ADTECH
b. AMAX
c. Advertising campaign
d. ACNielsen

3. A _________ is a relatively new executive level position at a corporation, company, organization typically reporting directly to the CEO or board of directors. The _________ is responsible for a brand's image, experience, and promise, and propagating it throughout all aspects of the company. The brand officer oversees marketing, advertising, design, public relations and customer service departments.

a. Financial analyst
b. Chief executive officer
c. Power III
d. Chief brand officer

4. The _________ is a global navigation satellite system (GNSS) developed by the United States Department of Defense and managed by the United States Air Force 50th Space Wing. It is the only fully functional GNSS in the world, can be used freely, and is often used by civilians for navigation purposes. It uses a constellation of between 24 and 32 Medium Earth Orbit satellites that transmit precise microwave signals, which allow _________ receivers to determine their current location, the time, and their velocity.

a. Power III
b. 180SearchAssistant
c. 6-3-5 Brainwriting
d. Global positioning system

5. In marketing, _________ has come to mean the process by which marketers try to create an image or identity in the minds of their target market for its product, brand, or organization. It is the 'relative competitive comparison' their product occupies in a given market as perceived by the target market.

Re-_________ involves changing the identity of a product, relative to the identity of competing products, in the collective minds of the target market.

a. GE matrix
b. Containerization
c. Moratorium
d. Positioning

Chapter 1

1. c 2. a 3. b 4. b 5. d 6. d 7. a 8. d 9. d 10. a
11. b 12. d 13. d 14. d 15. d 16. d 17. b

Chapter 2

1. d 2. c 3. d 4. a 5. a 6. b 7. c 8. a 9. c 10. a
11. d

Chapter 3

1. d 2. d 3. d 4. d 5. b 6. d 7. a 8. a 9. b 10. d

Chapter 4

1. c 2. c 3. d 4. b 5. a 6. d 7. d 8. b

Chapter 5

1. b 2. b 3. c 4. a

Chapter 6

1. d 2. d 3. d 4. b 5. b 6. a

Chapter 7

1. a 2. b 3. d 4. c

Chapter 8

1. d 2. d 3. d 4. d 5. b

Chapter 9

1. d 2. d 3. b 4. d 5. d

Chapter 10

1. d

Chapter 11

1. d 2. c 3. d 4. a 5. b 6. d 7. d 8. b 9. d 10. b
11. d

Chapter 12

1. d 2. d 3. d 4. c

Chapter 13

1. b 2. d 3. b 4. c 5. d 6. c 7. c 8. d 9. d 10. b
11. d 12. d 13. c 14. d 15. a 16. a 17. d 18. d 19. a 20. d
21. d 22. b 23. d

Chapter 14

1. d 2. c 3. d 4. d 5. d

www.ingramcontent.com/pod-product-compliance
Lightning Source LLC
Chambersburg PA
CBHW080744250426
43671CB00038B/2869
* 9 7 8 1 4 2 8 8 7 2 2 7 1 *